Uplook
for a
New Outlook

---

30 DAYS TO A NEW VIEW

RALPH DOUGLAS WEST, SR.

An Uplook for a New Outlook

30 DAYS TO A NEW VIEW

HUPOMONE PRESS
FORT WORTH, TEXAS

© 2016 by Hupomone Press, Fort Worth, Texas.
All rights reserved.
ISBN: 978-0-9982913-0-7
Printed in the United States of America.

Library of Congress Cataloging-in Publication Data-
An Uplook for a New Outlook 2016 /
Dr. Ralph D. West, Sr. 1960-

ISBN: 978-0-9982913-0-7

All Scripture quotations are taken from the New King James Version. Copyright © 1982 by Thomas Nelson, Inc. Used by permission. All rights reserved.

Contents

Introduction

Day 1 *Only One Way Out*
Day 2 *Your Mess Can Have Meaning*
Day 3 *Getting Up After You Have Fallen Down*
Day 4 *When the Best We Have Is Not Enough*
Day 5 *Turned on the Wheel, Fixed in the Fire*
Day 6 *Jesus Erases What the Enemy Defaces*
Day 7 *Exchange Weakness for Strength*
Day 8 *Wings of Lead*
Day 9 *A Second Touch*
Day 10 *A Future and a Hope*
Day 11 *Dreams, Detours, and Destiny*
Day 12 *A Token for the Journey*
Day 13 *Journeying Without a Map*
Day 14 *It's Time to Take a Risk*
Day 15 *Cross Over!*
Day 16 *Taking the Hard Place*
Day 17 *Breakout from Doubt*

Day 18 *Reverberations of Faith*
Day 19 *Giving God a Reason To Live Another Year*
Day 20 *Put Up the New Year's Tree*
Day 21 *Can We Change?*
Day 22 *Contact or Connection?*
Day 23 *Living the Surrendered Life*
Day 24 *Treasure in Jugs of Mud*
Day 25 *Nothing*
Day 26 *On the Tipping Point*
Day 27 *Take a Step Forward in Difficulty*
Day 28 *Take a Step Forward in Responsibility*
Day 29 *360 Thanksgiving*
Day 30 *The Wonderful Surprises of God*

Press On

Introduction

FROM ITS EARLIEST DAYS THE CHURCH has practiced a daily discipline of Scripture and reflection. The Dominican monks did it seven times a day, starting at four o'clock in the morning with regular breaks throughout the day of work and worship. If I woke up at 4 a.m. to do so, I would not say, "Good morning, Lord" but "Good Lord, it's morning." Life for you and me does not lend itself to such a practice. Yet life can have an achievable, sustainable, and sufficient time with the Lord as a matter of daily discipline. That is the purpose of this little book.

As you use the book, be sure you are *mindful*. There is a contemporary movement called mindfulness. To be mindful is to be in the moment, focused exclusively on what you are doing right now. If a person is in front of you, you are mindful of that person. If a task is at hand, you are fully invested in that task. Most of us are walking civil wars, divided within ourselves. We need to pray, but we think of the grocery list. We need to focus on Scripture, but we stop to send a text. The result is constant, endless distraction. We are never leaning in totally to what we are doing. We exercise and listen to a book; we talk on the phone and watch TV. Please let this little book be for 30 days a practice of mindfulness. Be in the moment as you focus on the two pages for each day.

Find a *place* that is sacred for this one purpose. We are creatures who associate activities with places. There is a place where we dress and undress. There is a place where we read the paper or sit to watch a game. Most of us sit in the same place to eat and feel misplaced if we have to move. Many of you sit in the same place at church. Having a sacred place for reading this book for 30 days will help you. Associate that place with 30 days of reading this little book.

Let that place be a *quiet* place. Most of us are uneasy with quietness. We particularly want music or the dull buzz of TV, even when we are not listening. For these 30 days please do all you can to find a quiet place to reflect on this book each day. That may not be possible at home; that is life. One friend sits in her parked car in the garage at work for 15 minutes to be quiet and alone with God before going in. If you want to you can find a quiet place somewhere. God spoke to Elijah in a still, small voice. Jesus got up a great while before dawn and went out into the desert. He did whatever He needed to do to find a place to get alone with God in the quiet. You can too.

From ancient times Christians have found it best to meet God *early*. What you do first sets the tone for the day. If you first watch the news, check your Facebook or email, and read the morning paper, you will find yourself distracted and spread thin. The voice that begins your day will set the direction for the day most of the time. The early presence of God sets the tone for the day; it is the background music for every encounter. Like the faint scent of a perfume, the fragrance of God wafts through your day. Jesus Himself got up a great while before daybreak. The psalmist indicated that God helped him just at the peep of dawn. The end of the day finds many of us exhausted and some of us discouraged. Meet God on the front porch of the day.

HOW TO USE THIS BOOK

This book is definitely not for speed reading. Years ago there was an advertising campaign for a speed-reading technique that enabled you to read a page in a few seconds. You were supposed to run your finger down a page, oscillating back and forth, and the advocates for the program said you had read the book! Needless to say, that is not the case. Just as there is a new emphasis on slow cooking, there should also be a new insistence on slow reading. These pages are not meant to be swallowed in a second like a morning pill. Rather, my thoughts here are for slow, meditative reading. Take your time. Focus on each word. Read the biblical text slowly several times. Ask yourself the following questions of the text related to each quote from me:

- Is there a warning here to heed?
- Is there a promise here to claim?
- Is there a requirement from the Lord for my life?
- How could I apply this today, this very day?

Ask the Holy Spirit to guide you in this. God wishes for you to seek the guidance of His Spirit, and He will not disappoint you when you ask Him to give that guidance. Let the pages of Scripture GLOW before you. Let the wind of the Spirit BLOW upon you. Then the circumstances of your life will FLOW with the Word and the Spirit.

TELL SOMEONE ELSE

Let the Lord lead you to someone at home, work, school, or rest who is responsive to spiritual suggestions. Briefly share with that person what the text for the day has meant to you. Do not preach a sermon. Just give a suggestion of what God has told you. You may introduce the conversation by saying, "This morning a thought came to me . . . . I was surprised when the Bible impressed me with . . . Sometimes you can be so surprised when God puts a new thought into your mind . . . Dr. West's remarks on life today arrested me . . . ."

Another use of this book involves having a brief family time over the 30 days. I know how pressed your life is. I definitely know how hard it is to get everyone together for any significant time at all. Perhaps you could take one week at a time. For that one week find some way to get everyone together for 10 minutes: at the table, before bedtime, in the midst of getting ready to go in the morning, or before everyone retires at night. Read the Scripture and page. Ask every family member to say the first thing that comes into their mind. It does not have to be profound or deep. Just ask everyone to respond. Say a brief prayer and ask God to lead your family deeper into the truth for that day.

KEEP A JOURNAL IN THE BOOK

This booklet is purposefully designed for you to write down the impressions on your spirit when you reflect on the reading. Again, this does not have to involve theological profundities. Just write down what the Spirit whispers to you. It may be a word, a name, a hymn, a situation, or an insight that at the moment seems unrelated. Write it down anyway. Later, after the 30 days, you will be surprised at what happened in your life as a result of those remarks written casually. God has a way of taking the impressions of the moment and turning them into the lasting and durable principles of a lifetime.

Let's get started right now. There is no wrong time to start. Do not let the Adversary tell you that this is not the time. Act right now. Seize the day. Don't procrastinate. Let's do the first day right now.

Ralph D. West, Sr.

DAY 1

Only One Way Out

WE ALL KNOW WHAT IT'S LIKE to have locked ourselves into our own mess. We've lifted up our fist and said, "God, I don't care what the counsel of Your Word says. I am going to do what I want to do!" At the time, we thought we were headed toward freedom, daylight, and good times. Instead, we sat in the darkness and gloom of our own isolated jail cell. We could not get up, and nobody wanted to help us up. There was no way out—on our own.

Here is news that is better than good: Grace is not just for those who accidentally stumble or lose their way. When we cry out to God, He breaks our chains and sets us free!

Stand fast therefore in the liberty by which Christ has made us free, and do not be entangled again with a yoke of bondage.

GALATIANS 5:1

Prayer Notes

Stop revisiting things and people and situations that God has already delivered me from —

Bondage

God has already broken those Chains I am Free

DAY 2

Your Mess Can Have Meaning

SOME OF US LIVE at the corner of Messy Avenue and Impossible Boulevard. Yet even in our impossible situation, there is a significant meaning in our mess. God will keep us in our mess until we learn the message in our unreasonable mess. Even though He is already planning our coming restoration, we may have to move into our mess for a season. In other words, we have to maximize our mess.

The best way to do this is by blessing our mess. The fact that we are in a messy situation doesn't mean we cannot ask God to bless others even in the midst of our mess. He will see us out of our mess, but He can bless us even in our mess.

Though the fig tree does not bud and there are no grapes on the vines, though the olive crop fails and the fields produce no food, though there are no sheep in the pen and no cattle in the stalls, yet I will rejoice in the Lord, I will be joyful in God my Savior.

HABBAKUK 3:17–18

Prayer Notes

Ask God to bless me even where I am in my mess

DAY 3

Getting Up After You Have Fallen Down

LIFE HAS OFFERED YOU nothing but a series of bitter disappointments. Weeping has endured for the night, and no joy has come in the morning. When this has happened to you, you must thirst for nothing less than the absolute reality of God and what He has meant to you. Remember those times when God was so near that nothing or no one was closer? These are the life-giving experiences that can sustain you when He seems so far away.

Getting back to God is the only way you can get back on your feet after you have been knocked down. Actually, the joy of Christian living is returning to God and finding in Him the nourishing refreshment to continue your spiritual journey with Him.

Blessed are those whose strength is in you, whose hearts are set on pilgrimage. As they pass through the Valley of Baka, they make it a place of springs.

PSALM 84:5–6

Prayer Notes

God has always lead me through smooth times and difficult times. I just keep my eyes fixed on Jesus + father god. P.s. I look to the hills from which comes my health an strength.

DAY 4

When the Best We Have Is Not Enough

IN THE COURSE OF LIFE, we encounter those impossible situations when our burdens are too heavy to carry, our problems too entangled for us to straighten out, and our anxieties too oppressive for us to bear. Only a power great and loving enough to lift what we cannot support, unsnarl what we cannot figure out, and relieve what we can no longer fight can get us through without disaster. Our confidence comes from knowing God, to whom we can give the burdens that are too great for the best we have. Like the mighty Niagara Falls that brings power where it's needed, in the Lord Jesus the vast resources of God are brought to the places where the best that we have is not enough.

"Come to Me, all you who labor and are heavy laden, and I will give you rest. Take My yoke upon you and learn from Me, for I am gentle and lowly in heart, and you will find rest for your souls. For My yoke is easy and My burden is light."

MATTHEW 11:28–30

Prayer Notes

Turning over all my problems and situations to the Lord and leaving them there. On this day and forever more

DAY 5

Turned on the Wheel, Fixed in the Fire

THAT WHEEL SPINNING us round and round under the Potter's hand represents the unpredictable circumstances of the days of our lives. Sometimes the wheel spins us around ecstasy and celebration, but other times it spins us around depression and deep despair. We're afraid our lives that are spinning out of our control will break us. Yet these very circumstances God will use to make us.

But then after spinning circumstances on the wheel of our lives, He fixes them within the fire of our trials. Some of you are experiencing physical, vocational, and domestic fires now and wondering why. Like the pottery that's only useful when it's strengthened through firing, until we are fixed in the fire, we are useless to serve Him and others.

> "Shall the clay say to him who forms it,
> 'What are you making?' Or shall your
> handiwork say, 'He has no hands'?"
>
> ISAIAH 45:9B

Prayer Notes

There is only One God and beside him there is no Other, it is he that made us and not we ourselves. Put no one before him, he is God by himself. No idols just One true and living God.

DAY 6

Jesus Erases What the Enemy Defaces

THE WORD "GRAFFITI" means "to be scratched or etched." Graffiti can be found in every language, everywhere. Sometimes it's just a tag for somebody to write their name. Other times distinctive graffiti marks off the territory of a gang. Even corporations have gotten into the act, hiring artists to write their names in graffiti.

God created you in His image for self-fulfillment, but the Enemy wants to write across you the graffiti of self-destruction. Right now, however, Jesus can erase what the Enemy has defaced in you because there is power in His unfailing Word and mighty name. Just as He did with the Gadarene demoniac, the Lord will cleanse you and restore the identity He originally gave you when you humbly confess your sin.

Therefore, if anyone is in Christ, he is a new creation; old things have passed away; behold, all things have become new.

2 CORINTHIANS 5:17

Prayer Notes

Accept Jesus Now, and forget/Repent of your past/and Jesus will forgive you, and Walk in the newness of the Spirit of God.

DAY 7

Exchange Weakness for Strength

ARE YOU RUNNING ON EMPTY? Do you go to bed tired, get up tired, and run tired all day long? Have you become quiet, sullen, or even withdrawn? Does God seem remote and disinterested to you? If these things are true of you, there is a powerful word about exchanging your weakness for God's strength from the prophet Isaiah.

Isaiah tells us in this verse to wait, renew, and soar. Waiting is not passivity, but an active, vigilant exercise that absorbs the power of God. The word "renew" suggests the exchange of our depletion for His donation of new strength. His strength leads to our soaring like an eagle above our disappointments. He matches the strength of His resources to the level of our need.

> *"The joy of the Lord is your strength."*
> NEHEMIAH 8:10

Prayer Notes

Amen — I'm waiting upon the Lord, for he will renew my strength & will rejoyce in him always!

DAY 8

Wings of Lead

OUR TEXT, IN ITS ORIGINAL CONTEXT and for us now, encourages those of us caught between the aspirations of what we would be as ministers and the real pressure of ministry that gives us lead wings. Paul gives us another outlook here. While we whine that our stress is so heavy it's killing us, he says that it's momentary and light. For him, glory is eternal and heavy. We should note that Paul does not mean an automatic relationship exists between trouble and glory. There is no alchemy that adds lead to trouble and turns it into the gold of glory. It is only GOD who can take tribulation and cause it to work out an abundant glory. GOD enables you not to lose heart.

Beloved, do not think it strange concerning the fiery trial which is to try you, as though some strange thing happened to you; but rejoice to the extent that you partake of Christ's sufferings, that when His glory is revealed, you may also be glad with exceeding joy.

1 PETER 4:12–13

Prayer Notes

Amen

Rejoyce in Knowing the God is in control over all lye and all its abundance and Glory.

DAY 9

A Second Touch

THIS BLIND MAN had to admit he needed another healing touch from the Lord. For the only time in His ministry, Jesus asked if something worked. Perhaps Jesus healed this man in two steps to keep the man's attention on Him so that he would cling to Him. If Jesus had done it all at once, this man might not have depended on Him.

You may say, "I see no way out." Yet you wouldn't be here now if God had not given you many ways out. You say, "I can't make it to the first of the month." But God has given you resources in the mail, refunds, dividends, closed accounts, inheritances, and friends you hardly knew. You need to get His second touch.

And my God shall supply all your need according to His riches in glory by Christ Jesus.

PHILIPPIANS 4:19

Prayer Notes

Trust and believe on
Jesus/God, and do not
weiver in your trust
and beliy.

Have faith & believe

DAY 10

A Future and a Hope

IN APPARENTLY HOPELESS CIRCUMSTANCES, Jeremiah affirmed a future and a hope with God. This prophet had a pious premonition that God was up to something hopeful. That prophecy came in the midst of his everyday affairs. We have definite, historical demonstration that Jeremiah's hope was well-founded. Seventy years after his words of hope in the midst of hopelessness, the people came back to the city. The walls, temple, and homes were rebuilt.

Through this prophet, we learn how to express hope—tangibly and sacrificially, obviously and memorably. Our hope for the future is not based on a Pollyanna kind of optimism, but a realism that believes in the promises of God. God also positively confirms our future through the well-founded hope of the open tomb.

Now faith is the substance of things hoped for, the evidence of things not seen.

HEBREWS 11:1

Prayer Notes

Have faith and believe.

DAY 11

Dreams, Detours, and Destiny

GOD DOES HAVE MORE WAYS than you think to use your imagination in speaking to you. Many of you believe the Christian message is *true*, but it isn't *real* to you. God can come to you in imaginative ways and make what is *true real*. He will even give you dreams regarding your individual destiny.

Along the journey to reach that destiny, God will allow you to experience detours like the Hebrews' Egypt before they traveled to the Promised Land. Egypt represents the detours that sometimes happen in the life of faith. Sometimes you will find yourself off the mainline and on the sideline. But rest assured that nothing and no one—personal foibles or demons—can hinder the purpose of God in your life.

He who calls you is faithful, who also will do it.

1 THESSALONIANS 5:24

Prayer Notes

Amen.
God has his way of bring
things to past that even with
the necked eye might show
you apprent - "Trust God
Plan" always. I'm
"Living By Faith"

DAY 12

A Token for the Journey

IMAGINE WHAT HAPPENS when you're driving down a lonely highway and you "put the pedal to the metal" and the motor dies. Or perhaps you're looking for "vroom," but you're living on fumes. Is there anything more frightening than traveling on unfamiliar, desolate roads without having enough fuel?

Life has a way of draining your joy, your dreams, your position, and your power. So how do you make it when you are on empty? The Holy Spirit is the certain source of fueling when you are running on empty. As the passenger in your journey to the future, He knows you are running on empty. The transforming Spirit of hope forces you to get back at it, refuel for the road, and keep on the journey.

"Not by might nor by power, but by My Spirit," says the Lord of hosts.

ZECHARIAH 4:6

Prayer Notes

Leaning on The Lord for everything. Never lose faith

DAY 13

Journeying Without a Map

LIKE A SHIP ON A MYSTERY VOYAGE sailing under sealed orders, we all start out in life traveling to a place we know not where. It will be revealed later. Meanwhile we must go out in faith, journeying under sealed orders without a map. In like manner, all the pioneers of faith have ventured out, not knowing where they were going—but going nonetheless.

Security with God never means sitting still or remaining static. Instead, it means moving continually on the way to some goal beyond the present that beckons to us but has yet been unattained. The symbol of this kind of faith would be a hoisted sail, not an anchor. The goal is "a promised land" out ahead, not a haven of rest.

So Abram departed as the Lord had spoken to him, and Lot went with him. And Abram was seventy-five years old when he departed from Haran.

GENESIS 12:4

Prayer Notes

On a Journey with my Lord and Savior Jesus Christ

DAY 14

It's Time to Take a Risk

WHAT IS IT ABOUT TAKING RISKS that excites us and at the very same time makes us fearful? We seem to be in love with the idea of risks if somebody else is taking the risk. While only a brave or crazy few are daring enough to take chances, the rest of us watch in awe, shaking our heads and exclaiming, "Boy, look at that!" Whatever the reason, we like the idea of taking risks—to a certain extent, that is.

How willing are you to take a risk for the sake of Christ? Our Christian lifestyle has become awfully lame and same and tame. We may begin to wonder, "Does Christ expect normal, average me to risk something for Him?" The answer is yes.

> *"Have I not commanded you? Be strong and of good courage; do not be afraid, nor be dismayed, for the Lord your God is with you wherever you go."*
>
> JOSHUA 1:9

Prayer Notes

Don't be afraid to risk it all for the God who gives us all that we can ask or think He is the One and only Mighty God

DAY 15

Cross Over!

IN THE OLD TESTAMENT a great crossing changed the destiny of the people of God forever—the Hebrews' crossing over of the Jordan River in the days of Joshua. The generation that had wandered in the wilderness for 40 years made the decision to cross the Jordan River into the Promised Land. It required the people to commit to God's leadership and be willing to follow the will of God.

When you prepare to cross over a river in your life, you also need the certainty of divine direction. If you keep your eyes on the Jordan, you will be so paralyzed, you'll never move. But when you keep your eyes on the manifest presence of God, you can move when you see God move.

For I know the thoughts that I think toward you, says the Lord, thoughts of peace and not of evil, to give you a future and a hope.

JEREMIAH 29:11

Prayer Notes

Keep your eyes on Jesus
And He will direct your Path.

DAY 16

Taking the Hard Place

DEEP IN THE HEART, hidden in the secret places, everyone faces life's challenges by choosing one of two basic attitudes. One is to shun and shirk and loiter and lurk in the easy places. The other is to dare to do the difficult, take the hard places, and occupy the hard ground.

What choices do you make daily—at home, work, school, play? At the church and the gym, in travel and in leisure, are you willing to dare to do the difficult? Just as the most valuable pearls require the most dangerous diving, so also does life require of us. Jesus said it well, "Whoever seeks to save his life will lose it, but whoever loses his life for My sake shall find it."

> "Do not fear nor be afraid of them; for the Lord your God, He is the One who goes with you. He will not leave you nor forsake you."
>
> DEUTERONOMY 31:6

Prayer Notes

Taking life difficult times yet you are not alone. God is ever present and a constant help in times of troubles.
You - I am Never Alone

DAY 17

Breakout from Doubt

JUST AS CHRISTIAN in *Pilgrim's Progress* is thrown into the dungeon of Doubting Castle where Despair lives, many of us are also living in that depressing place where we have lost our joy and song. When we're physically exhausted, socially isolated, or emotionally rejected, it will certainly discourage our faith in God.

But the good news is that we don't have to stay there. We must first send ourselves to Jesus when we doubt. He only and always gives faith. He is the source of love, power, and a sound mind. Moreover, Jesus will do whatever it takes to give us the evidence we need to live free of doubt. We can escape Doubting Castle by unlocking its door with the key of His Word.

> "For assuredly, I say to you, whoever says to this mountain, 'Be removed and be cast into the sea,' and does not doubt in his heart, but believes that those things he says will be done, he will have whatever he says."
>
> MARK 11:23

Prayer Notes

Believe "Always" even when it seems like it can not happen just believe and give it to God in Prayer.

DAY 18

Reverberations of Faith

THE WRITER OF HEBREWS says a curious thing about Abel: "By faith he speaks, even though he is dead." The faith of Abel is reverberating from the grave. Abel never said a recorded word while alive, but he has evidently become loquacious after death. How does Abel speak after his death? Do we want to say what countless funeral sermons have said about this text? The good works of a righteous person, in this case Abel's, continue to speak long after the person who performed them is gone. Certainly that is the primary reason Abel's name appears in this list of the faithful. We can admire his faith, learn from it, and imitate it. In this way Abel, though dead, still speaks to subsequent generations.

The righteous man walks in his integrity; his children are blessed after him.

PROVERBS 20:7

Prayer Notes

With faith All things are possible.

DAY 19

Giving God a Reason To Live Another Year

WHAT DIFFERENCE DOES IT MAKE whether you live or die? Other than your friends, relatives, and acquaintances who will be heartbroken by your absence, what difference will you really make? What is your reason for wanting to live another year? Today, if you could appeal before God for another year, what would be your reason for living?

What is your reason for hanging around here? Can God, when He hears you pray, say, "There is sincerity on those lips"? Can God speak of your integrity? That is, do you act the same way in public as you do in private? Can God depend on you when He cannot depend on those around you? You can give God grounds for giving you more time to live.

See then that you walk circumspectly, not as fools but as wise, redeeming the time, because the days are evil.

EPHESIANS 5:15–16

Prayer Notes

Walking in love + light with my faith to always do right and a woman of integraty

DAY 20

Put Up the New Year's Tree

EVERYONE KNOWS ABOUT putting up Christmas trees, but no one has ever set out a New Year's tree. For those of us making a fresh start in life, we don't have to wait until January 1st of next year to plant a sturdy tree that has its roots in the soil of Psalm 1. It involves establishing our lives by a source that will sustain us for all our years on earth—and all eternity.

When you fly over west Texas and look at the desert, you can always tell where the rivers flow. Trees on their banks are growing strong and tall. In the same way, God wants us to plant the trees of our lives by His life-giving waters that continually sustain us.

*That they may be called trees of
righteousness, the planting of the Lord, that
He may be glorified.*

ISAIAH 61:3

Prayer Notes

I've/I'm planting the soil of my life in the Hands of Jesus and his Father, which is my father and being one w/ the body of Christ. One day @ a time.

DAY 21

Can We Change?

NAAMAN FACED A SITUATION beyond human help. Even though he was a mighty man of valor in a great empire, he had one thing no emperor could help him with—leprosy. How often even the competent, strong, affluent, educated, and successful wrestle with something that is beyond all of their vaunted human effort. God uses an unlikely process, washing seven times in the lowly Jordan, to heal him.

In our hearts we have demons that we cannot defeat on our own. But like arrogant Naaman, many of us think we know better than God's way to change—through our education, credentials, positions, prominence, and achievement. Nevertheless, God commands us to go wash in the blood of Calvary, the most repellent thing for the self-confident individual.

> "God resists the proud, but gives grace to the humble."
>
> JAMES 4:6

Prayer Notes

I have been washed by the blood of Jesus. and I stand by faith know every thing is going to be alright.

DAY 22

Contact or Connection?

WITH TWO KIND OF INDIVIDUALS, God either uses the saw or the pruning shears. In this passage Jesus talks about those withered branches the vinedresser takes away and throws into the fire. The warning here is that we may be in contact with the life of Christ in religiosity but not in true connection with Him. The Father takes away such fruitless branches with the saw.

In wintertime the vinedresser removes some shoots with pruning shears to make other shoots more fruitful. God is the vinedresser who prunes away our prideful shoots so that we might be more fruitful. Often we make an idol of our spiritual feelings instead of worshiping Him. Yet He will strip away our spiritual pride until we are left with Him alone.

*As many as I love, I rebuke and chasten.
Therefore be zealous and repent.*

REVELATION 3:19

Prayer Notes

Ooh To Be Prunned and Picked/Choosen by God is the Best thing life has to offer/give.

DAY 23

Living the Surrendered Life

WHAT GOD WANTS TODAY from His children is new men and women, rather than new methods—surrendered people, rather than just saved people, for it is possible to be saved yet not surrendered. As the believer maintains an attitude of surrender, a daily change takes place in his life, described in this text both positively and negatively.

"To be conformed" means "to be like, or take the shape of." The surrendered believer is no longer conformed to the policies, fashions, and practices of the world about him. Instead, a distinctiveness of lifestyle sets him apart from the natural and carnal man. So many Christians are like chameleons that change their color according to their surroundings; you cannot tell the difference between them and the unconverted.

Do not love the world or the things in the world. If anyone loves the world, the love of the Father is not in him.

1 JOHN 2:15

Prayer Notes

Surrendering my life to God.

And being transformed by the Holy Spirit not this world.

DAY 24

Treasure in Jugs of Mud

IN THAT ANCIENT WORLD it was very common to keep expensive, valuable treasure in worthless, unattractive clay jars. What Paul has in mind is for us to see the contrast in an incongruity. We have a treasure in a ceramic pot, a clay jar. The great reality is that we do have a treasure—the gospel of Christ.

Have you ever said, "I am too weak for God to use me"? Consider the possibility that you are not weak *enough* for God to use you. When we pretend we are something more than clay jars, then God can never make His strength conspicuous in us. God conquers in those lives that know all too well they are nothing but clay jars with a treasure inside.

For by the grace given to me I say to everyone among you not to think of himself more highly than he ought to think, but to think with sober judgment, each according to the measure of faith that God has assigned.

ROMANS 12:3

Prayer Notes

Amen
Stop pretending and
Surrender your whole
life to Christ.

DAY 25

Nothing

BUT WHAT ABOUT THE FUTURE? Can anything arise that will threaten our relationship with the Lord? Who can separate us from the love of Christ? This does not involve our love for Christ but Christ's love for us. Our capricious, fickle kind of love can run hot and cold and almost turn into ashes. Yet Paul emphasizes that nothing shall separate us from Christ's love for us.

Indeed, no state of existence can separate us from Christ. He begins with death, the greatest and ultimate enemy. According to Paul, to die is only to receive more of Christ (Philippians 1:23). Also, no invisible, supernatural power, no span of time or space, or "anything else in all creation" can come between Christ's love and the believer.

> *"And lo, I am with you always, even to the end of the age."*
>
> MATTHEW 28:20B

Prayer Notes

Nothing can seperate me from the love of Jesus Christ.

DAY 26

On the Tipping Point

THERE WOULD BE NO HIGH MOUNTAINS like Everest and K-2 without valleys. Abraham and Jacob represent titanic mountain peaks in the history of Jehovah's dealings with His people. Isaac, on the other hand, is like a valley between two mountain peaks, representing the obedient and submissive qualities of an equable trust in God.

And yet, Isaac seemed to live on the tipping point between faithfulness and failure. He did have the spiritual sense to re-dig the wells his father Abraham dug. On the other hand, just like his father, he defensively lied to the Pharaoh about his wife. Today we can choose which legacy of our family members to follow in our own lives—whether to renew their past faithfulness or reflect their past failures.

If, however, he begets a son who sees all the sins which his father has done, and considers but does not do likewise; ...he shall surely live!

EZEKIEL 18:14, 17B

Prayer Notes

Most times paving out your own way in our adult life gives us a far greater feel of accomplishment know we done it our selves marking out our own blueprint

DAY 27

Take a Step Forward in Difficulty

MAXIMUM DIFFICULTIES, such as long-term illness of a family member or other stressful disruptions of normal everyday living, can occur at any time. For the most part, under these circumstances the sufferers are exempt from many normal responsibilities. For example, people facing those trials would not be expected to have lavish parties at their houses.

Although we admit that difficulties do not keep us from meeting our legal obligations, some of us feel that any difficulty, even a minor one, provides an excuse not to give to the work of God. Indeed, it takes grace to give out of difficulty. We must choose to be like the early Macedonian church, who, despite their crushing impoverished state, were astonishingly generous toward the Jewish Christians in Jerusalem.

> *"Truly I say to you that this poor widow has put in more than all; for all these out of their abundance have put in offerings for God, but she out of her poverty put in all the livelihood that she had."*
>
> LUKE 21:3–4

Prayer Notes

Giving from the Heart, is worth more, than given from a boastful Person

DAY 28

Take a Step Forward in Responsibility

WE HAVE HABITS in every area of life. Personal hygiene, work, and the payment of bills are all matters of principle and habit in the life of any normal person. In fact, we live by habit, except in our spiritual lives. Yet God also wants us to live by some *holy habits*.

He desires us to plan with commitment, purpose, and determination that which we will give to Him on a regular basis. Certainly God deserves the same discipline we reserve for the utility and mortgage companies. We should not wait for a certain spirit, impulse, or some special need to move us to give. Instead, we must give with planned regularity. In fact, the Scriptures emphasize that giving is the responsibility of every Christian.

Bring all the tithes into the storehouse, that there may be food in My house.

MALACHI 3:10A

Prayer Notes

He require the first fruit of your labor 10%

DAY 29

360 Thanksgiving

JACK WELCH WAS THE CEO OF GE and a well-known corporate leader. He led a 360 review for all of his 300,000 employees. Everyone evaluated those above them, alongside them, and below them in the organization. He fired the bottom 10% each year. That was a 360-degree evaluation that resulted in loss.

The oldest book in the New Testament, 1 Thessalonians, refers to another 360 evaluation that gives grounds for thanksgiving. How quickly we revert to an attitude of entitlement. Yet all that we have is a gift of God—from the air we breathe to the vastness of the universe beyond. Beyond all material blessings, we should be thankful that our life has deep resources given to us by the abundant grace of God.

*Oh, give thanks to the Lord, for He is good!
For His mercy endures forever.*

1 CHRONICLES 16:34

Prayer Notes

I give thanks to God for all that he has done will reveil to me and continues to do in my life

DAY 30

The Wonderful Surprises of God

GOD IS A GOD of wonderful surprises. The amazing, almost unbelievable consequence of faith in God is to find that He is able to do abundantly above all that we ask or even think. Always beyond our expectations, God is able to bring every equation into balance. As Christians, our joy centers in the discovery that just when life has weighted the equation against us, God appears with power that strikes victory in the heart of defeat. He lifts up hope out of despair.

There is no situation that God cannot use in some way for His good purpose. For in everything God works for good with those who love Him. God's purposes will prevail, and this promise enables us to endure in the meantime.

> *"Behold, I am the Lord, the God of all flesh.
> Is there anything too hard for Me?"*
>
> JEREMIAH 32:27

Prayer Notes

No there is never anything to hard for my God. He supplies all our needs, according to his riches in Glory

Press On

DO IT AGAIN

When I was a little boy, my favorite story was "Miss Ticklefeather's Puffin Paul." It was a silly book about a lady and her bird. I could never get enough of the book. When my parents had read it, I immediately asked them to read it again, right then. I would never get to hear it as many times as I wanted. To this day, decades later, I remember virtually every word of the book.

When my parents grew weary, they would sometimes try to change a word or scene in the book. Immediately, I resisted. That book was ingrained into my young personality. I always asked them, "Do it again."

There is value in repetition. In the midst of the last century, John Baillie wrote *A Diary of Private Prayer,* which has sold millions of copies. It has prayers for every day of the month, morning and evening. Millions of people have read those prayers for years. The cadence of the words, the personal notes in the margin, and the comfort of the prose is like putting on an older sweater or pair of house shoes. It just makes you feel at home with the LORD. You start over with the beginning of each new month and read them again.

This book can become like that. When you have finished reading it for 30 days, put it down for a week and then do it again. Read the notes you have made in your journal. You will be shocked at what God has done in your life that you would have forgotten without those notes. If you want to, read the book from the last day back to the first. Or start in the middle and go both ways. Read the book out loud. Vary your discipline and you will be surprised at the different effects.

We need spiritual discipline. We brush our teeth, change our oil, take out our trash, and pay our mortgage with discipline. Does God not deserve the same repetition of discipline that we bring to mundane, worldly tasks?

Make it a priority of discipline to reread this book. Tie it to something you do every day. Read it when you put your feet on the floor in the morning. Or read it before you turn out the light at night. And then do it again the next month. Make notes each time. If you write in black ink one month, right in green ink the next. Date your notes.

The ancient rabbis considered careful reading of divine things an act of worship. When you focus on these words and read them prayerfully, you are engaged in the deepest level of worship. Let these daily readings and the Spirit of God lead you into all truth.

And remember, Pas will be reading this with you. I will also be recording these readings and making them available in my own voice on our church website. That way, you can read along with me as I read the words for both you and me. We are in this thing together until He comes.

Ralph. D. West, Sr.

Notes